■SCHOLASTIC

writing guides

With interactive resources on CD-ROM

Fantasy Stories

for ages
9–11

Maggie Beard and
Louise Carruthers

Terms and conditions

**IMPORTANT – PERMITTED USE AND
WARNINGS – READ CAREFULLY BEFORE USING**

Credits

Authors
Maggie Beard and
Louise Carruthers

Development Editor
Simret Brar

Editors
Roanne Charles and
Marion Archer

Assistant Editor
Pam Kelt

Series Designer
Anna Oliwa

Designer
Paul Stockmans

Cover Illustration
Mark Oliver

Illustrations
Sarah Warburton and
Mike Phillips

CD-ROM Development
CD-ROM developed in
association with Infuze Ltd

Text © Louise Carruthers, Maggie Beard
© 2009 Scholastic Ltd

Designed using Adobe InDesign

Published by Scholastic Ltd,
Villiers House,
Clarendon Avenue,
Leamington Spa,
Warwickshire
CV32 5PR

www.scholastic.co.uk

Printed by Bell & Bain

1 2 3 4 5 6 7 8 9   9 0 1 2 3 4 5 6 7 8 9

British Library Cataloguing-in-Publication Data
A catalogue record for this book is available from the British Library.

ISBN 978-1407-11270-1

Acknowledgments
The C S Lewis Company for the use of an extract from *The Lion, the Witch and the Wardrobe* by C S Lewis © 1950, C S Lewis (2002, HarperCollins).
Random House Group for the use of an extract from *The Snow Walkers Son* by Catherine Fisher © 1993, Catherine Fisher (1992, The Bodley Head).

CD-ROM Minimum specifications:

Windows 2000/XP/Vista		Mac OSX 10.4
Processor: 1 GHz	RAM: 512 MB	Graphics card: 32bit
Audio card: Yes	CD-ROM drive speed: 8x	Hard disk space: 200MB
Screen resolution: 800x600		

Mixed Sources
Product group from well-managed forests and other controlled sources
www.fsc.org Cert no. TT-COC-002769
© 1996 Forest Stewardship Council
FSC

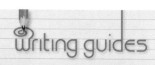

Contents

Introduction: Fantasy Stories

The *Writing Guides* series aims to inspire and motivate children as writers by using creative approaches. Each *Writing Guide* contains activities and photocopiable resources designed to develop children's understanding of a particular genre (for example, fairy stories). The activities are in line with the requirements of the National Curriculum and the recommendations in the *Primary Framework for Literacy*. The teacher resource books are accompanied by a CD-ROM containing a range of interactive activities and resources.

What's in the book?

The *Writing Guides* series provides a structured approach to developing children's writing. Each book is divided into four sections.

Section 1: **Using good examples**

Three text extracts are provided to explore the typical features of the genre.

Section 2: **Developing writing**

There are ten short, focussed writing tasks in this section. These are designed to develop children's ability to use the key features of the genre in their own writing. The teacher's notes explain the objective of each activity and provide guidance on delivery, including how to use the photocopiable pages and the materials on the CD-ROM.

Section 3: **Writing**

The three writing projects in this section require the children to produce an extended piece of writing using the key features of the genre.

Section 4: **Review**

This section consists of a 'Self review', 'Peer review' and 'Teacher review'. These can be used to evaluate how effectively the children have met the writing criteria for the genre.

What's on the CD-ROM?

The accompanying CD-ROM contains a range of motivating activities and resources. The activities can be used for independent work or can be used on an interactive whiteboard to enhance group teaching.

Each CD-ROM contains:

- three text extracts that illustrate the typical features of the genre
- interactive versions of selected photocopiable pages
- four photographs and an audio file to create imaginative contexts for writing
- a selection of writing templates and images which can be used to produce extended pieces of writing.

The interactive activities on the CD-ROM promote active learning and support a range of teaching approaches and learning styles. For example, drag and drop and sequencing activities will support kinaesthic learners.

Talk for writing

Each *Writing Guide* uses the principles of 'Talk for writing' to support children's writing development by providing opportunities for them to rehearse ideas orally in preparation for writing. 'Talk for writing' is promoted using a variety of teaching strategies including discussions, questioning and drama activities (such as, developing imaginative dialogue – see *Fantasy Stories for Ages 9–11*).

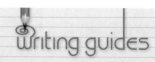

How to use the CD-ROM

Start screen: click on the 'Start' button to go to the main menu.

This section contains brief instructions on how to use the CD-ROM. For more detailed guidance, go to 'How to use the CD-ROM' on the start screen or click on the 'Help' button located in the top right-hand corner of the screen.

Installing the CD-ROM

Follow the instructions on the disk to install the CD-ROM onto your computer. Once the CD-ROM is installed, navigate to the program location and double click on the program icon to open it.

Main menu screen

Main menu

The main menu provides links to all of the writing activities and resources on the CD-ROM. Clicking on a button from the main menu will take you to a sub-menu that lists all of the activities and resources in that section. From here you have the option to 'Launch' the interactive activities, which may contain more than one screen, or print out the activities for pupils to complete by hand.

If you wish to return to a previous menu, click the 'Menu' button in the top right-hand corner of the screen; this acts as a 'back' button.

Screen tools

A range of simple writing tools that can be used in all of the writing activities are contained in the toolbar at the bottom of the screen.

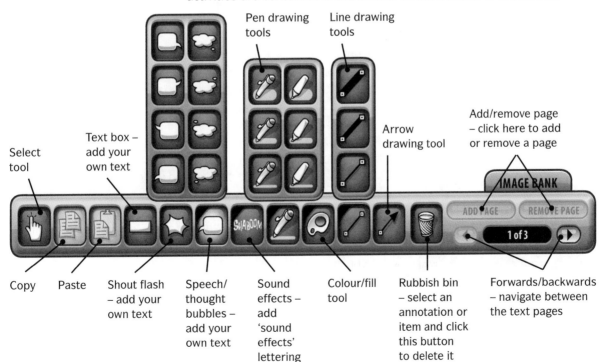

Pen drawing tools

Line drawing tools

Text box – add your own text

Select tool

Arrow drawing tool

Add/remove page – click here to add or remove a page

Copy

Paste

Shout flash – add your own text

Speech/ thought bubbles – add your own text

Sound effects – add 'sound effects' lettering

Colour/fill tool

Rubbish bin – select an annotation or item and click this button to delete it

Forwards/backwards – navigate between the text pages

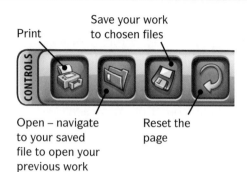

Print

Save your work to chosen files

Open – navigate to your saved file to open your previous work

Reset the page

Printing and saving work

All of the resources on the CD-ROM are printable. You can also save and retrieve any annotations made on the writing activities. Click on the 'Controls' tab on the right-hand side of the screen to access the 'Print', 'Open', 'Save' and 'Reset screen' buttons.

View all thumbnails by clicking on the arrows

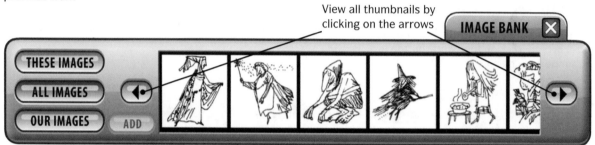

Image bank – click and drag an image to add it to an activity

Image bank

Each CD-ROM has an 'Image bank' containing images appropriate to the genre being taught. Click on the tab at the bottom right of the screen to open the 'Image bank'. On the left-hand side there are three large buttons.

- The 'These images' button will display only the images associated with the specific activity currently open.
- The 'All images' button will display all the photographs and illustrations available on the CD-ROM.
- The 'Our images' button will contain any images you or the children have added to the CD-ROM.

Press the left or right arrows to scroll through the images available. Select an image and drag and drop it into the desired location on the screen. If necessary, resize the image using the arrow icon that appears at the bottom right of the image.

You can upload images to the 'Image bank', including digital photographs or images drawn and scanned into the computer. Click on 'Our images' and then 'Add' to navigate to where the image is stored. A thumbnail picture will be added to the gallery.

Writing your own story

Each CD-ROM contains a selection of blank writing templates. The fiction genre templates will be categorised under the button 'My story' and the non-fiction templates will be categorised under 'My recount' or 'My writing'. The writing templates encourage the children to produce an extended piece of genre writing. They can also add images, speech bubbles and use other tools to enhance their work.

The fiction titles also include a cover template for the children to use. They can customise their cover by adding their own title, blurb and images.

Section 1
Using good examples

Fantasy story features

Settings
- Imagined worlds with fantasy landscapes, people and creatures; their own rules, customs, languages and rituals
- Sometimes two-world settings, starting in the real world.

Characters
- Imagined creatures or ordinary people
- Archetypal characters: protagonist (hero), antagonist (villain), helpers, guide.

Structure
- Simple linear chronology
- Complex non-linear chronology, eg parallel narratives or flashbacks.

Plot
- Typically a quest with high and low points.

Language features
- Detailed description, figurative language and imagery
- Temporal connectives.

Fantasy stories

Fantasy is a popular narrative genre that is well represented in children's literature, television programmes, films and computer games. In addition, many popular fantasy stories also have their own websites which children can visit to find out more about the fantasy genre. Try www.harrypotter.warnerbros.com and www.narnia.co.uk.

Typically, fantasy stories are action-packed tales of mythical creatures, imagined worlds, magic and the battle of good versus evil. Some fantasy stories, such as *The Hobbit* by JRR Tolkien or *The Snow-Walker's Son* by Catherine Fisher are set entirely in a fantasy world and have a straightforward linear chronology. Two-world fantasy stories such as *The Chronicles of Narnia* by CS Lewis and the Harry Potter series by JK Rowling have more complex narrative structures as the characters move through time and space in different ways.

A multimedia approach

In addition to shared reading of a range of appropriate fantasy texts, a wide variety of other media can be used as stimulus for children's writing. The strong motivational effect of ICT, films and visual texts and images make them ideal starting points to inspire creative writing.

The prevalence of the fantasy genre in computer games make them a fantastic tool for motivating boys, in particular, to engage with the writing process. Computer games can be used to explore key aspects of the fantasy genre including typical plots, characters and settings. For example, like most fantasy novels, many computer games are based on a quest and so can be used to develop children's understanding of narrative structure and provide ideas for children's independent writing.

Links to the Primary Framework

The popularity of the fantasy genre in its various forms makes it an ideal starting point for developing various aspects of children's writing, including compositional skills, grammatical skills, vocabulary knowledge and spelling skills, as well as creativity and imagination. In Years 5 and 6 there are also a number of opportunities to teach children specifically about different aspects of the fantasy genre, for example, Year 5 Narrative Unit 1 'Novels and stories by significant children's authors' and Year 6 Narrative Units 1 and 2 'Fiction genres' and 'Extending narrative'.

Extract 1: The Lion, the Witch and the Wardrobe

What's on the CD-ROM

The Lion, the Witch and the Wardrobe
- Text extract to read and discuss.

This extract introduces an example of a two-world fantasy story where characters move from the real world to a parallel fantasy world.

- Open the extract on the CD-ROM or hand out copies of photocopiable page 10. Read Extract 1 with the children and ask them to identify the genre. Briefly discuss familiar fantasy stories and elicit that many operate in two worlds (the real world and an imagined world), with a 'doorway' or portal that connects them. Ask the children to explain the two worlds and the portal in this story.

- Examine how the author uses descriptive language to create a picture of the fantasy setting. Explain that, typically in two-world stories, the real world is mundane and the fantasy world is extraordinary. Discuss why.

- Explain the three key aspects to a setting – time, place and climate. Discuss these and come up with a few examples of each.

- Hand out copies of photocopiable page 13, 'Settings: a two-world story', and ask the children to create and describe a real world and a fantasy setting for their own two-world fantasy story.

Extract 2: The Snow-Walker's Son

What's on the CD-ROM

The Snow-Walker's Son
- Text extract to read and discuss.

Making a fantasy villain
- Rollover each heading to display text prompts.
- Complete the table by analysing how a character is brought to life.

This extract demonstrates how techniques in dialogue, atmospheric description and action can be used effectively in characterisation.

- Display Extract 2 and read it together on screen. Ask the children if they can use the extract to predict which roles Gudrun, Jessa and Thorkil fulfil in the story (villain, hero and guide) and to explain, with reference to the text, why they think as they do.

- Encourage the children to comment on the overall effectiveness of this extract. How does it make them feel? Would they like to read on? Why/why not? Highlight Jessa and Thorkil's initial reactions to and observations of Gudrun (for example 'Jessa had never felt so afraid.') and discuss how these observations work to intensify the reader's reaction to Gudrun and contribute to the atmosphere of foreboding.

- Organise the children into pairs, and hand out copies of photocopiable page 11 'The Snow-Maker's Son', along with photocopiable page 14 'Making a fantasy villain'. Ask the children to explore the different techniques in description (of setting as well as character), action and dialogue that Catherine Fisher uses to build an image of Gudrun in the reader's mind.

- In a feedback session, open the CD-ROM file 'Making a fantasy villain' and follow the instructions to record some of the children's suggestions. Roll over the headings for ideas.

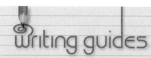

Extract 3: Jacob's Quest

This extract illustrates how figurative language can be used to describe the places, people and objects in a fantasy story.

- Display Extract 3 on screen or hand out copies of photocopiable page 12 and read the text together. Ask: *What impact does the extract have? What effect is the author trying to achieve?*

- Focus on the title of the story. Explain that in many fantasy stories the plot centres around a quest or journey. Ask the children to refer to the extract to establish who Jacob is and the purpose of his quest.

- Examine the different techniques used to depict the fantasy setting. Ask them to underline adjectives, verbs and adverbs that describe sights and sounds, and type in alternatives. Highlight evidence of the character's reaction to the atmosphere, for example, how it affects his body, behaviour and thoughts.

- Encourage the children to identify and discuss the similes. What is being described and what is it being compared to?

- Divide the class into small groups. Give each group a copy of photocopiable page 15 'Simile starters' and ask them to match each picture to the correct simile starter. Reveal the correct answers using the activity 'Simile starters' on the CD-ROM.

- Open the 'Setting similes' file on the CD-ROM and complete the examples. Alternatively, ask them to complete photocopiable page 16.

Poster: Fantasy stories

- Display the 'Fantasy stories' poster on the whiteboard. Explain to the children that the poster provides a summary of the characteristic features of the fantasy genre. Explore and discuss each section of the poster, remembering to hover over each area to display further details about each aspect of the genre. Alternatively, hand out copies of photocopiable page 18, 'Fantasy stories', and discuss examples of plot, character and setting.

- Ask the children to share some fantasy stories that they are familiar with from books, film or television (even computer games, if appropriate). Encourage them to identify and explore examples of the features represented on the poster.

- Organise the children into pairs and hand out copies of photocopiable page 17, 'Looking at fantasy stories'. Begin by examining the extract from *The Lion, the Witch and the Wardrobe*.

- You can also use the poster as a planning/evaluation tool to support independent writing. The children can use photocopiable page 17 as a reminder and prompt sheet to ensure they include all the key features of the genre when creating their own fantasy stories.

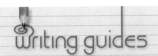

Section 1: Using good examples

Extract 1: The Lion, the Witch and the Wardrobe

It is raining. Lucy, Edmund, Susan and Peter have just finished breakfast and begin to explore the big house they are staying in. The first room they look in is empty except for a wardrobe. The others leave because there is nothing of interest but Lucy decides to climb in amongst the fur coats...

Soon she went further in and found that there was a second row of coats hanging up behind the first one. It was almost quite dark in there and she kept her arms stretched out in front of her so as not to bump her face into the back of the wardrobe. She took a step further in – then two or three steps – always expecting to feel the woodwork against the tips of her fingers. But she could not feel it.

'This must be a simply enormous wardrobe!' thought Lucy, going still further in and pushing the soft folds of the coats aside to make room for her. Then she noticed that there was something crunching under her feet. 'I wonder if this is more moth-balls?' she  thought, stooping down to feel it with her hand. But instead of feeling the hard, smooth wood of the floor of the wardrobe, she felt something soft and powdery and extremely cold. 'This is very queer,' she said, and went on a step or two further.

Next moment she found that what was rubbing against her face and hands was no longer soft fur but something hard and rough and even prickly. 'Why, it's just like branches of trees!' exclaimed Lucy. And then she saw that there was a light ahead of her; not a few inches away where the back of the wardrobe ought to have been, but a long way off. Something cold and soft was falling on her. A moment later she found that she was standing in the middle of a wood at night-time with snow under her feet and snowflakes falling through the air.

From *The Lion, the Witch and the Wardrobe* by CS Lewis

Extract 2: The Snow-Walker's Son

Behind them, someone had come into the Hall, someone silent, without footsteps, someone who froze the air. Jessa felt sudden crystals harden on her face and mouth; felt a cold numbness that pierced her skin. Thorkil was still; frost glistened on his lips.

'It's Gudrun,' he breathed.

And as if the walker on the stairs had heard him, the footsteps stopped, and began to come back down.

Suddenly, Jessa had never felt so afraid. Her heart thudded; she wanted to run, had to fight to hold herself still, clenching her fingers into fists. Before them the footsteps came closer; behind in the Hall some terrible coldness loomed.

Someone was sitting in the Jarl's chair, looking no more than a bundle of rich fabrics. Then he pushed his hood back, and Jessa saw it was a very old man, thin and spry, his hair wisps of white, his look sly and sidelong.

'They leave tomorrow,' he was saying. 'As you expected.'

Astonished, Jessa stared at Thorkil.

The woman laughed, a low peal of sound that made a new surge of fear leap in Jessa's stomach.

The old man chuckled too. 'And they know all about Thrasirshall, the poor waifs.'

'What do they know?' she said.

'Oh, that the wind howls through it, that it's a wilderness of trolls and spirits on the edge of the world. Not to speak of what the Hall contains.' He spat, and then grinned.

They could just see the woman's white hands, and her sleeves. Gently, Thorkil edged the curtain a little wider.

Gudrun stood in the light from the window. She was tall and young, her skin white as a candle; her hair pure blonde and braided in long intricate braids down her back. Her ice-blue dress was edged with fur. Silver glittered at wrist and throat; she stood straight, her sharp gaze towards them. Jessa felt Thorkil's instant stillness. Even from here, they could see her eyes had no colour.

From *The Snow-Walker's Son* by Catherine Fisher

Text © 1992, Catherine Fisher.

Section 1: Using good examples

Extract 3: Jacob's Quest

Jacob took a deep breath and raised his right hand to grab the heavy brass door knocker. Even on tiptoes he could only just reach it and he had to concentrate hard to hold on as he swung it back and forth against the rough, wooden door that towered above him. Bang. Bang. Bang. Each knock made the floor beneath him shake like an earthquake, and the birds, which just a few moments before had been singing happily, fell silent.

After everything he'd been through to get to the castle it seemed a little ridiculous to be knocking at the door, but there was no other way in. Every other doorway and window was barred or blocked up – it looked like a prison.

Jacob's mouth turned dry and his stomach churned like the clothes in his mum's washing machine as he thought about what he might find on the other side of the door. Even the sky seemed to get darker, as if the sun had sensed something terrible was about to happen and decided to hide its face behind the clouds.

He wanted to run away, but he couldn't let Kristie down. He had to get inside to help her.

Suddenly, the door began to open, swinging back slowly to reveal a long, stone corridor. Candles flickered on the walls, like little boats with golden sails floating in the darkness. Water dripped slowly from the ceiling.

Jacob felt for his sword, which had protected him so well until now, and taking strength from the familiar object he stepped inside.

As his eyes adjusted to the darkness he saw something move at the end of the passageway. There was a horrible scream, like someone scraping their nails down a blackboard, and then a shadow, half-animal, half-human, began to hurtle towards him.

This was it...

Illustration © 2009, Mike Phillips.

Settings: a two-world story

● Compare the settings in a two-world fantasy story.

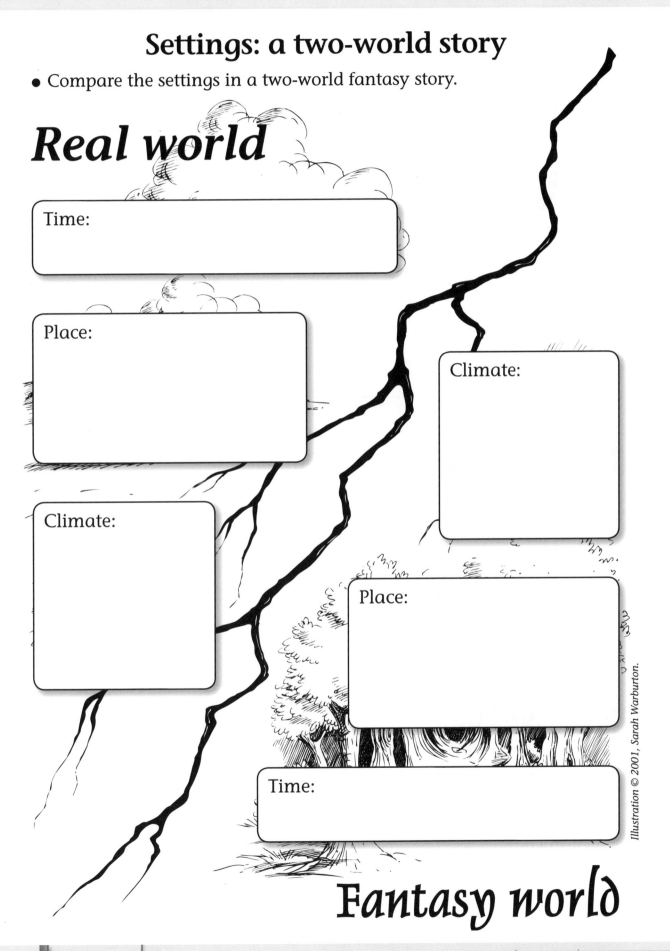

Real world

Time:

Place:

Climate:

Climate:

Place:

Time:

Fantasy world

Illustration © 2001, Sarah Warburton.

Photocopiable ◼SCHOLASTIC
www.scholastic.co.uk

Making a fantasy villain

● Look at the extract from *The Snow-Walker's Son*. Explore how the author presents the character Gudrun using dialogue, description and action. Note down your ideas in the table below.

Action

- What does Gudrun do?
- What do you learn about Gudrun from the actions of Jessa and Thorkil?

Dialogue

- What does Gudrun say?
- How does she speak?

Description

- What words and phrases describe Gudrun's appearance and character?

Simile starters

● Cut out the cards and match the pictures to the sentences.

The stars sparkled like	Inside the cave it was as black as	The dragon's eyes glowed like
The rain fell from the sky like	The waves crashed like	The monster's teeth were as sharp as

rubies

diamonds

tears

knives

night

cymbals

Illustration © 2009, Mike Phillips.

Setting similes

A simile is a comparison between two things, using 'like' or 'as'. For example:

The polar bear was as white as snow.

The stars sparkled like diamonds.

● Write a list of similes to describe this setting.

Illustration © 2009, Mike Phillips.

The moon shone in the sky like _____

_____

The night was as black as _____

_____

The forest was as creepy as _____

_____

● Now turn over and write some similes of your own.

Looking at fantasy stories

- Talk about other fantasy books, films or TV programmes, then complete this grid with a partner.

Fantasy story	One world or two?	Settings (there may be one or two)	Characters and their roles (hero, villain, guide)	Portal (only used in two-world stories)	Reason for the journey or quest
The Lion, the Witch and the Wardrobe					

Illustrations © 2001, Sarah Warburton.

fantasy stories

plot	character	setting

plot

Fantasy objects

Conflict and resolution

Quest or journey

character

Fantasy creatures

Helpers

Guide

Villain

Hero

setting

Doorway/portal

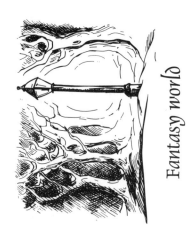

Fantasy world

Real world

writing guides

Section 2

Developing writing

In this section, children develop key genre features in their own writing in preparation for writing a complete fantasy story.

How to use the activities

The activities in this section offer the children imaginative ways to explore the conventions of the fantasy genre. The accompanying teaching notes explain the purpose of each activity and give guidance on delivery, including how to use the photocopiable pages at the end of the section and the interactive materials on the CD-ROM.

A range of different teaching approaches is suggested in order to help the children to gain new skills and to stimulate ideas which are then developed through individual, paired and whole-class work. It is best if all of the activities are modelled as shared writing and/or guided writing activities before the children are asked to work independently.

Developing genre writing

The short, focused writing tasks outlined in this section are designed to support and scaffold the development of specific elements of the children's fantasy story writing, including:

- the use of descriptive language (including figurative language) to develop fantasy settings

- how to develop characterisation using action, description and dialogue to build and present archetypal fantasy story characters

- different narrative techniques that can be used to engage and entertain the reader and create particular effects, such as building suspense

- developing understanding of different fantasy story structures and plot features such as parallel narratives and a quest pattern.

Developing imaginative ideas

It is also vital to develop the children's imagination and encourage creativity. Where appropriate, the teacher's notes outline how resources such as books, films, television programmes and the children's own experiences can be used to fire their imaginations and generate ideas they can draw on when they come to plan and write a complete fantasy story of their own.

Activities breakdown

Activity 1: Wanted – a hero...

Objective

To use varied vocabulary to create effects appropriate to form and purpose. Maintain style (Year 6 Strand 9 Writing target).

What to do

The children complete an application form for a job as a fantasy hero.

- Ask the children to recall typical attributes of a fantasy hero. Encourage them to express personal opinions about characters from their own reading. Ask: *Who is your favourite fantasy hero? Why do you like them? What makes them good at their job?*

- Now hand out copies of photocopiable page 25 'Wanted – a hero'. Discuss possible responses and encourage the children to let their imaginations run wild! Make some suggestions to set the ball rolling. Demonstrate how to present information in the formal style appropriate to a job application form.

- Now ask the children to fill in an application form of their own, drawing a picture of themselves as the hero. Encourage them to think about what skills the advertisement is asking for as they complete it.

- You could develop this activity further in speaking and listening (drama) by holding job interviews in which children take on the role of the hero they have created and present persuasive arguments for why they should be given the job.

Activity 2: Introducing the guide

Objective

To create characters in writing using action, description and dialogue (Year 5 Strand 9 Writing target).

What's on the CD-ROM

Introducing the guide
- Drag and drop a selected image of the guide.
- Create a character profile for the guide.

What to do

Here the children introduce a typical fantasy story character using action, description and dialogue.

- Ask the children to recall archetypal characters found in fantasy stories (hero, villain, guide, helpers) and the qualities they would expect each character to possess.

- Focus on the role of 'guide'. Make a list of the names of guides from fantasy books and films the children know. Consider what common characteristics these guides have (for example, wisdom and special knowledge) and what the main purpose of the role is (to provide the hero with advice and support at significant points in the story).

- Explain to the children that you would like them to write a section of a fantasy story in which the guide is introduced. Revisit Extract 2 (see page 11) to recap on characterisation.

- Work together to complete the plan 'Introducing the guide' on the CD-ROM. You may use the image of the guide from the 'Image bank' or upload your own (see 'Help file' for instructions). Then in shared writing use the plan to write a few paragraphs for a fantasy story. Model how to use description, dialogue and action to develop characterisation.

- Using photocopiable page 26 'Introducing the guide', ask the children to plan and write about their own fantasy guide.

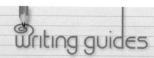

Activity 3: In the fantasy world

Objective

To use adventurous vocabulary to describe setting, mood and characters (Year 5 Strand 9 Writing target).

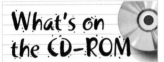

What's on the CD-ROM

The Lion, the Witch and the Wardrobe, and Jacob's Quest
● Example extracts.

In the fantasy world
● Create a word bank of descriptive and figurative words and phrases.

Media resources
● Use the 'Rock caves' photograph as a stimulus for writing.

What to do
The children describe a setting as experienced by the main character.

● Read Extracts 1 and 3 (on the CD-ROM or pages 10 and 12). Consider why description is such an important feature of this genre. (Many fantasy stories use imaginary settings and characters that the reader needs to visualise.)

● Ask the children to recall some of the different techniques used by authors to describe story settings. (For example, literal description of sights and sounds, figurative language, reporting a character's response to a setting.)

● Display the 'Rock caves' image from the 'Media resources' section of the CD-ROM. Ask the children to imagine that they have been transported from the classroom into this fantasy setting. Ask the children to describe the setting and, referring to all the senses, how it makes them feel. Encourage the use of adventurous vocabulary including precise adjectives, powerful verbs, adverbs and similes.

● Open the CD-ROM file 'In the fantasy world' and record ideas.

● In shared writing, model how to use the bank of words to describe a setting through the eyes of the main character (as in Extract 1).

● Then ask the children to complete photocopiable page 27 'In the fantasy world', using the same or another photograph.

Activity 4: Fantasy kingdom

Objective

To use varied vocabulary to create effects appropriate to the form and purpose of the writing (Year 6 Strand 9 Writing target).

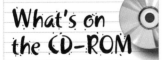

What's on the CD-ROM

Fantasy kingdom
● Drag and drop symbols to create a map of a fantasy kingdom.

What to do
This activity creates a map of a fantasy setting.

● Show the children a fantasy novel which contains a map(s) of its world (such as *The Hobbit*) and elicit that the map gives visual reality to the imaginary world and helps the reader to track the journey. Consider the appearance of the map. For example, does it look old-fashioned, contemporary or futuristic? Discuss how the effect is created.

● Display the CD-ROM file 'Fantasy kingdom' and establish what the symbols represent. Work together to drag and drop the symbols onto the map. Label the features and the kingdom itself with imaginative names invented by the children.

● Ask a volunteer to mark on the map a route that passes through each of the different places. Imagine a fantasy hero follows this route. Consider: *What might happen to the hero in each location? Who will he or she meet? What obstacles and challenges will he or she face?*

● Hand out copies of photocopiable page 28 'Fantasy kingdom' and ask the children to create a kingdom for their story. They should include at least five locations, including the villain's home and the hero's background.

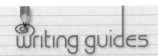

Activity 5: Opening chapter

Objective

To organise ideas into clear sections/paragraphs with an appropriate opening and closing (Year 5 Strand 10 Writing target).

What to do

This activity helps the children to open a two-world fantasy story.

- Remind the children that a key feature of the fantasy genre is the use of a 'doorway' or 'portal' that transports the main character from the real world into the fantasy world, and back again. Ask the children to recall the portals in stories they have read, such as Platform 9¾ in the Harry Potter books and the rabbit hole in *Alice in Wonderland*. Notice that in spite of their magical powers, portals are usually unremarkable features of the real-world surroundings. Discuss reasons for this, such as building suspense and adding an element of surprise.

- Hand out copies of photocopiable page 29 'Opening chapter'. Discuss various contrasting settings and suitable objects to move characters between worlds.

- Now work together to use the settings and portal to plan the opening chapter of a two-world fantasy story. Encourage the children to make notes about what to include in each paragraph. Explain how to organise and develop the notes into paragraphs. Describe a cliffhanger ending that leaves the story at a critical point, adding an element of suspense, and ask the children to think of one of their own.

Activity 6: Fantasy objects

Objective

To use different narrative techniques to engage and entertain the reader (Year 6 Strand 9).

What's on the CD-ROM

Fantasy objects
- Drag and drop marbles and create magical powers for each of them.
- Write about how the magic powers of one marble effect events in a story.

What to do

This creative activity gives the children the opportunity to turn an everyday object into a fantastic object with special powers.

- Make a list of fantasy objects from stories the children have read (for example, the invisibility cloak in the Harry Potter books).

- Ask the children to describe each fantasy object and explain what it does. Consider the *role* of the object in the story. Perhaps the hero embarks on a quest to recover it or uses it to assist him or her on the journey. Stress that the objects are simply everyday items that have been given special powers.

- Open the CD-ROM file 'Fantasy objects'. Begin by dragging the marble images from the 'Image bank' on to screens 1 and 2. Together, assign a special power to each marble. Then decide which marble to use in their story. Ask the children to work in pairs to imagine they have just taken this marble out of the bag. What happens to them? Do they use their new powers for good or evil? Share ideas as a class.

- Ask the children to work on photocopiable page 30 'Fantasy objects' individually or in their pairs. Remind them that they are writing about magical powers and exciting events/action, so they will need to use a range of adjectives and powerful verbs and vary the length of their sentences.

Activity 7: The quest

Objective

To adapt non-narrative forms and styles to write fiction or factual texts (Year 5 Strand 9).

What to do

In this activity, the children draw on their knowledge of fantasy themes to devise the plot for a new story.

- Tell the children that they are going to devise the plot for a new fantasy story with a quest. Referring to Extracts 1, 2 and 3 (pages 10–12) and other familiar fantasy stories, elicit plot structures and themes characteristic of the genre (for example, good versus evil, a quest with a series of events that builds up to conflict then resolution).

- Give out enlarged copies of photocopiable page 31 'The quest'. Explain about how to move along the board, reading the squares. Note that the start and finish points of the game represent the beginning and end of the story and that the spaces in between record details of events (highs and lows) that build up to a showdown scene (conflict and resolution) at the end of the story.

- Work together to come up with suggestions to be written into the empty spaces.

- Ask the children in pairs to develop the plot for their own fantasy quest. They can swap boards with another pair and play the game.

Activity 8: Showdown!

Objective

To vary pace and develop viewpoint through the use of speech, action and detail (Year 5 Strand 9).

What to do

Many fantasy quests end with a showdown between hero and villain. In this activity, the children will describe one such battle of good versus evil.

- Read or watch several examples of climactic battles from suitable sources. Discuss the impact of the scenes and explore the dramatic effects each author or film-maker was trying to achieve (such as fear, suspense, excitement). Identify different narrative techniques that draw in the reader (such as, short sentences, using a question to involve the reader, snappy dialogue, adventurous vocabulary, cliffhanger paragraphs or scene breaks).

- Display an enlarged version of photocopiable page 32 'Showdown!' Ask the class to select elements to create a hero and a villain and to suggest the cause of conflict between them.

- In shared writing, compose the defining battle between the two characters. Encourage the children to use description, action and dialogue to make the narrative both scary and exciting. Reflect critically on the piece, then help the children to edit and improve it (for example, by better word choices, detailed action and more believable dialogue).

- Now give out copies of photocopiable page 32 'Showdown!' to each child and ask them to plan, write and edit their own description of a battle between the two opponents.

Activity 9: Building suspense

Objective

To use different narrative techniques to engage and entertain the reader (Year 6 Strand 9).

What's on the CD-ROM

Building suspense
- Rollover the dragon image to reveal writing tips.
- Write a paragraph which builds suspense.

Media resources
- Use the 'Fire breathing dragon' image as a stimulus for writing.

What to do

In this activity, the children look at different narrative techniques to build suspense in advance of describing a significant event.

- Open the CD-ROM file 'Building suspense'. Rollover the image of the dragon to reveal five writing tips for them to consider. Then, as a class discuss the different techniques used to build suspense, such as the use of short, dramatic sentences and adverbs.

- Display the 'Fire breathing dragon' image from the 'Media resources' section of the CD-ROM and ask the children to imagine they are about to come face to face with this terrifying creature. Ask: *What do you notice first?* (Perhaps a burst of flames, a plume of smoke.) *How do you feel?* (Terrified, heart pounding, legs trembling…) *What do you do?* (Run for your life? Advance nervously?)

- Together, in the 'Building suspense' CD-ROM file, write a short paragraph about this encounter, using the writing tips to help build suspense.

- Hand out copies of photocopiable page 33 'Building suspense' for the children to complete independently.

Activity 10: What did they say?

Objective

To punctuate sentences accurately, including use of speech marks and apostrophes (Year 5 Strand 11).

What's on the CD-ROM

Media resources
- Listen to and discuss the audio clip.

What to do

This activity explores the use of dialogue in fantasy stories and revises speech marks and other dialogue punctuation.

- Using Extract 2 (page 11) and other short excerpts from fantasy novels or films, focus on the use of dialogue in fantasy narratives. Identify the main purpose of the dialogue in each extract (for example, to explain part of the plot, to aid characterisation, to build tension, to entertain).

- Play the audio clip from the 'Media resources' section of the CD-ROM. Then ask: *What is happening in the story? What do we learn about the characters and the relationship between them?*

- Display an enlarged version of photocopiable page 34 'What did they say?'. Read the dialogue together. Revise the use of speech marks and other forms of sentence punctuation by asking the children to help you put in the missing punctuation.

- Ask the children to take on the roles of Josh and Sam to continue the dialogue. Encourage them to develop the plot and show how the characters react to events. Evaluate how well each pair uses dialogue to move the plot on and how their performance conveys the characters' feelings and reactions.

- Hand out copies of photocopiable page 34 'What did they say?' for the children to complete independently or in pairs.

 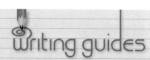

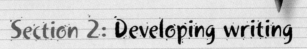
Wanted – a hero...

● Fill in this form to apply for the job of fantasy hero.

Name: _____

Age: _____

Qualifications: _____

_____

_____

_____

Previous experience:

_____

_____

_____

_____

Interests:

_____

_____

_____

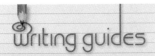

Introducing the guide

- Create your own fantasy guide using the planner below.

Description

- Draw and label a picture of your guide.

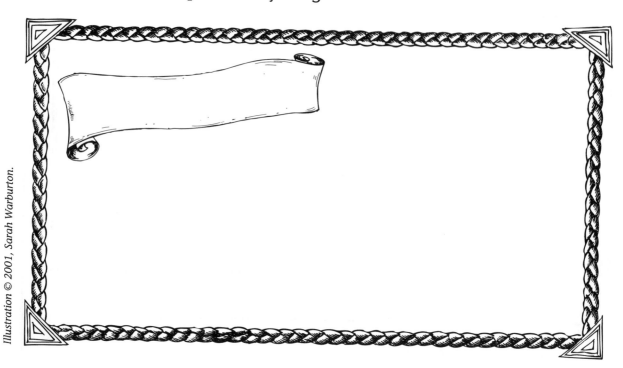

Illustration © 2001, Sarah Warburton.

Action

- Plan how the guide becomes involved in the story.

_____

_____

_____

_____

_____

Dialogue

- Plan something the guide will say.

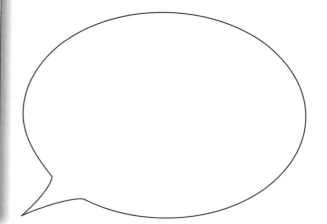

- Write a paragraph describing the moment your guide meets the hero you created in Activity 1. Use description, action and dialogue to introduce your fantasy guide. Use a separate piece of paper or the back of this sheet.

In the fantasy world

● Look carefully at the 'Rock caves' photograph in the 'Media resources' section of the CD-ROM. Imagine you are there. Create a bank of words and phrases to describe the setting.

Adjectives	Powerful verbs
Adverbs	**Similes**

● Now describe the setting as experienced by the hero you created earlier.

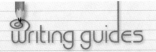

Fantasy kingdom

- Design your own fantasy kingdom. Draw and label key features on the map.

KEY

swamp	
mountains	
forest	
ruins	
village	
cave	
river	
volcano	
castle	

Illustrations © 2009, Mike Phillips.

Opening chapter

● Plan the opening chapter for a two-world fantasy story. First, choose a real-world setting, a fantasy setting and a portal to move between them.

Portal

Real world   **Fantasy world**

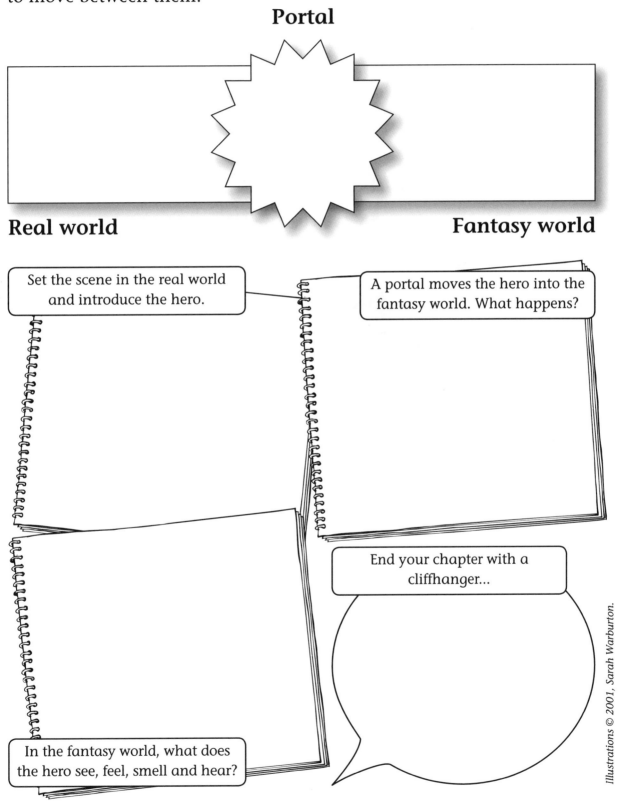

Set the scene in the real world and introduce the hero.

A portal moves the hero into the fantasy world. What happens?

End your chapter with a cliffhanger...

In the fantasy world, what does the hero see, feel, smell and hear?

Illustrations © 2001, Sarah Warburton.

Fantasy objects

● These are fantasy marbles. Write an explanation of each marble's special power.

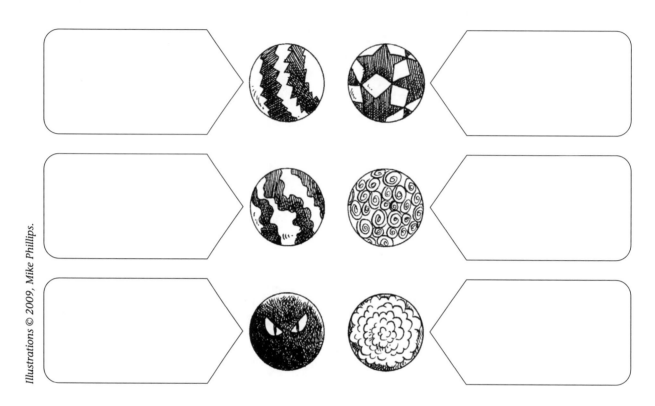

Illustrations © 2009, Mike Phillips.

● Choose one of the marbles to use in a story. Write notes about how this marble's special powers effect events in the story.

_____

_____

_____

_____

_____

_____

_____

writing guides

The quest

● Develop the plot for your own fantasy quest story by completing the sections below.

1 START	2	3	4	5
				6
	The quest			7
17 FINISH	16 SHOWDOWN	15	14	8
		13		9
		12	11	10

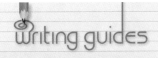

Showdown!

● Think about your hero and villain. Plan a final battle of good versus evil.

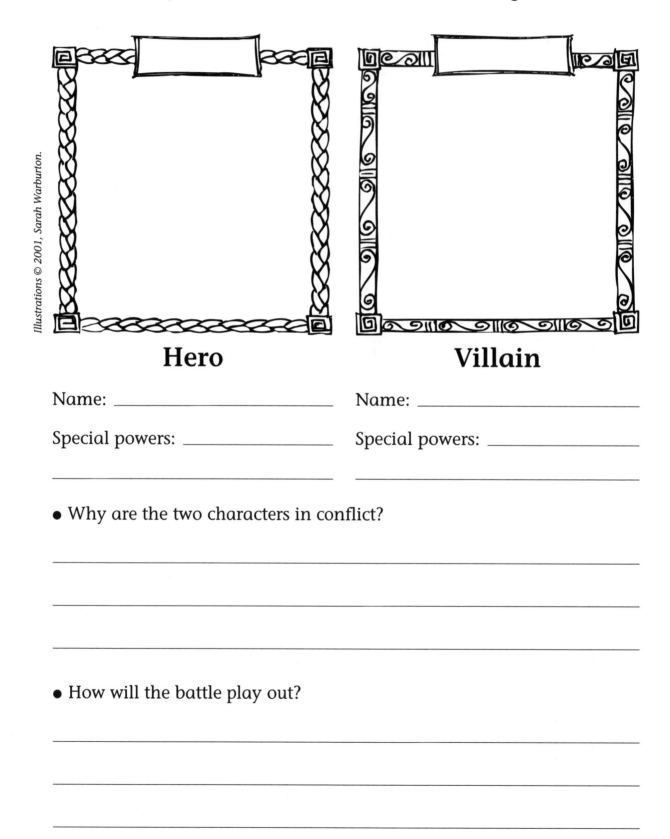

Illustrations © 2001, Sarah Warburton.

Hero

Villain

Name: _____   Name: _____

Special powers: _____   Special powers: _____

_____   _____

● Why are the two characters in conflict?

_____

_____

_____

● How will the battle play out?

_____

_____

_____

Building suspense

● Imagine you are the hero of a fantasy story. You are about to come face to face with the dragon. Using the five tips below, make notes and then write a paragraph that builds suspense.

1. Use short dramatic sentences.

2. Use a question to draw the reader into events.

3. Create a hostile setting.

4. Use connectives such as 'suddenly' or 'without warning' to inject suspense.

5. Describe characters' thoughts, feelings and reactions.

Illustration © 2009, Mike Phillips.

What did they say?

● Read the dialogue carefully. Put in the missing punctuation.

Come on whispered Sam Let's just have a quick peek and see what Grandpa keeps inside his shed He yanked the door open and was blinded by a blaze of white light...

Oh no! What's happening cried Sam and Josh as the ground opened up and they felt themselves falling through the air

Ouch! I've landed on something sharp yelled Sam

Serves you right said Josh crossly dusting himself down after the fall Grandpa told us not to look in the shed Now look what you've done You're always getting me into trouble

It's awfully hot down here... Where do you think we are said Sam apprehensively

How do I know It's so dark I can't see anything I knew we shouldn't have opened the shed door moaned Josh

Sam turned around and saw a bright light flashing in the distance Look at that light perhaps that's the way out I'll go and have a look said Sam boldly

I'm coming with you Josh called I'm not stopping here on my own this place is giving me the creeps

Suddenly the sound of footsteps and a large bang startled them both...

Hold on what was that exclaimed Sam Who's there

At last I've been waiting for you said a booming cackling voice I wondered when you would come...

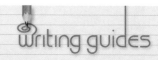

Section 3

Writing

The three extended writing projects in this section provide opportunities for the children to put everything they have learned about writing fantasy stories into practice.

Each of the projects requires the children to plan and write a complete fantasy story using narrative structures characteristic of the genre.

- In Project 1, 'Introduction to another world', the children plan and write a simple chronological narrative set entirely in a fantasy world.

- Project 2, 'Back and forth', and Project 3, 'My fantasy story', both require the children to plan and write two-world fantasy stories in which the characters move through time and space, but in different ways. When they are completing these writing tasks, it might be appropriate to encourage the children to experiment with more complex narrative structures with non-linear chronology, such as parallel narratives and time-shift techniques.

When writing their extended stories, the children will be helped to organise their writing into paragraphs or chapters and to use connecting words and phrases to create links between paragraphs and to indicate changes in time or place.

Providing support

In order to progress from initial ideas to finished stories, the children will require a number of extended writing sessions. It is important to provide targeted support for all children during independent writing to help them to plan, draft, edit and improve their stories.

It is recommended that all of the children are given a copy of photocopiable page 18 'Fantasy stories' to remind them of the characteristic features of the fantasy genre when they are planning and writing their fantasy stories.

The children should also have access to their work from previous lessons and be encouraged, where appropriate, to incorporate into their extended writing the imaginative ideas they developed in Sections 1 and 2.

Using the writing templates

The writing templates provided on the CD-ROM allow the children to produce their own fantasy stories using images and text. The templates can be used in two ways. The children can type their stories directly into the templates and then save and print their work. Alternatively, the blank layouts can be printed for the children to fill in by hand. (This may be particularly useful for drafting and editing, for example.) As well as a writing frame, the templates include several additional features, for example, in enabling children to design a book cover for their story.

Writing tips

- Create typical fantasy characters, settings and events.
- Develop characters by describing what they do, say, think and feel.
- Use adjectives, adverbs, powerful verbs, similes and metaphors to describe people, places, objects and events.
- Use connectives to link events, build suspense and shift attention.
- Include questions to involve the reader.
- Use 'story ingredients': opening, build-up, challenge, events, resolution and ending.

Project 1: Introduction to another world

Objective

To use different narrative techniques to engage and entertain the reader (Year 6 Strand 9).

What's on the CD-ROM

Media resources
- Use the 'Northern Lights' and 'Fire breathing dragon' images as stimulus for writing.

Character cards
- Type details onto cards to create characters.

My fantasy story
- Compose an introduction using the writing templates.

What to do

For this project, taking inspiration from a photograph, the children start to plan and write a simple chronological narrative set in a fantasy world, starting with a powerful introduction.

- Display the 'Northern Lights' photograph from the 'Media resources' section of the CD-ROM. Encourage the children to suggest a range of words and phrases, including figurative language, to describe the setting. Remind them to talk about time, place, weather and climate. Ask: *Who lives here? Are they good or evil? What is about to happen?*

- Open the CD-ROM file 'Character cards' and set the children to work on individual computers or on photocopiable page 38 to create the main character/s for their story.

- Some fantasy stories contain creatures, so display the 'Fire breathing dragon' image from the 'Media resources' section of the CD-ROM. Discuss this creature and the role it could play in a fantasy story. Then hand out copies of photocopiable page 39 'Fantasy creatures' and encourage the children to answer the questions and create their own fantasy creature.

- Once they have made their characters (hero, villain, creature and so on), ask the children to think of a challenge that the main character will face and consider how it will be overcome. Allow the children to discuss their ideas with a partner.

- Now the children have their setting, characters and basic plot idea, hand out copies of photocopiable page 40 'Writing an introduction' and discuss the key points. Can the children come up with any more aspects of how to write a compelling introduction?

- Tell the children to look closely at the first page of their favourite fantasy story. Explain that good introductions have a 'hook' to grab the reader's attention. Ask: *What is the 'hook' in their chosen story? Why does it work?*

- Next, load 'My fantasy story' and click on a blank layout to open a page. In shared writing, choose one of the children's story ideas to compose and write an attention-grabbing opening paragraph.

- Explain that you would like the children to start writing their introduction to their own fantasy story using the templates on the CD-ROM.

- Before they start, demonstrate how to add text and insert and resize images from the 'Image bank' then save and retrieve work.

- Remind the children about how to structure their work, with sentences and paragraphs to organise the order of events and to develop the action.

- Once they have completed their introduction, ask the children to read and evaluate their own, editing it as appropriate, then share it with a partner. Ask: *Can you guess what happens next?*

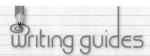

Project 2: Back and forth

Objective

To experiment with different narrative forms and styles to write their own stories (Year 5 Strand 9).

What's on the CD-ROM

Media resources
- Use the 'Museum artefacts' image as a stimulus for writing.

Fantasy object factfile
- Describe a fantasy object.

Story plan
- Complete a plan.

My fantasy story
- Compose a story using the writing templates.

What to do

This project is about incorporating a magical object into a two-world fantasy story. It offers an opportunity for children to try a narrative with non-linear chronology.

- Display and discuss the 'Museum artefacts' photograph of the golden chalices in a museum, from the 'Media resources' section of the CD-ROM. Encourage the children to share experiences of visiting museums. What kind of treasures and mysterious objects did they see?

- Using the 'Fantasy object factfile' on the CD-ROM or photocopiable page 41, ask the children to choose an object to use in their story. Explain that they can refer to the work they produced in the Section 2 activity 'Fantasy objects' (see page 22). Ask them to describe the object in detail using a range of adjectives, similes and metaphors.

- Now ask the children to work the setting and object into a fantasy narrative using the 'Story plan' on the CD-ROM or photocopiable pages 42 and 43. Then give them time to develop the plan into their own fantasy story, using the 'My fantasy story' writing frame.

- Support children to experiment with complex narrative structures, such as flashbacks. Model how to organise paragraphs and use connectives to help the reader understand what is happening, where and when.

Project 3: My fantasy story

Objective

To use varied structures to shape and organise text coherently (Year 6 Strand 10, Step in learning 3).

What's on the CD-ROM

Story plan
- Complete a plan.

My fantasy story
- Compose an extended story using the writing templates.

What to do

For this project the children will write a full, extended fantasy narrative, incorporating as many elements of the fantasy genre as possible.

- Open the CD-ROM file 'Story plan', in the 'Planning' section. Recap the different elements and the typical structure of a fantasy story. Remind the children of their previous work and to draw on their knowledge of quest-style computer games to generate exciting, imaginative ideas.

- Invite the children to add their ideas to the boxes. Alternatively, supply copies of photocopiable pages 42 and 43 'Story plan' for them to fill in.

- Next, open the 'My fantasy story' writing frame on the CD-ROM and browse the various templates together. Ensure the children know how to key in words, delete them and insert images.

- Ask the children to create their own fantasy story, using the 'My fantasy story' writing frame. Encouraged them to produce a story of a substantial length (at least two or three chapters).

- Once children begin writing, they may think of new ideas or want to make changes. Encourage them to use the 'Story plan' as a working document on which to make notes. The children could role play scenes from their stories to help develop ideas and to try out story dialogue.

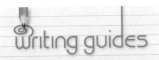

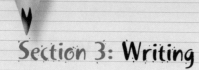
Character cards

● Look at the 'Northern Lights' photograph in the 'Media resources' section of the CD-ROM. Use the cards below to create the main characters for a story that takes place in this fantasy land.

Name: _____

Age: _____

Role in story: _____

_____

Appearance: _____

_____

Personality: _____

_____

Special power(s): _____

_____

_____

Name: _____

Age: _____

Role in story: _____

_____

Appearance: _____

_____

Personality: _____

_____

Special power(s): _____

_____

_____

Fantasy creature

● Do fantasy creatures inhabit your fantasy world? Use the 'Fire breathing dragon' image in the 'Media resources' section of the CD-ROM as inspiration to create a fantasy creature for your story.

Creature's name: _____

Is the creature real or mythical?
(e.g. unicorn, dragon, phoenix, vampire, werewolf)

Is it good or evil?

Can it speak? If so, what does it say?

Where does it live?

Draw your fantasy creature.

What does it eat?

Describe its appearance.

Photocopiable ■SCHOLASTIC
www.scholastic.co.uk

Writing an introduction

● Complete the web diagram to create an exciting opening to your story.

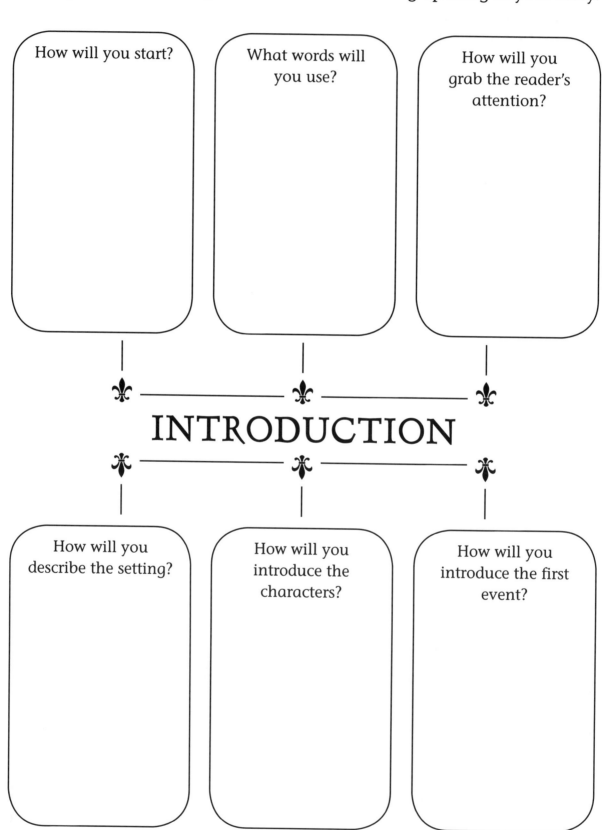

How will you start?

What words will you use?

How will you grab the reader's attention?

INTRODUCTION

How will you describe the setting?

How will you introduce the characters?

How will you introduce the first event?

writing guides

Fantasy object factfile

● Choose one of the objects to use in your story and using the questions below describe it.

_____

_____

_____

_____

_____

_____

_____

_____

_____

How old is it?

Who did it belong to?

What is it made of?

Where did it come from?

Illustrations © 2009, Mike Phillips.

Story plan

● Plan your fantasy story and make notes about any changes you would like to make to your story drafts.

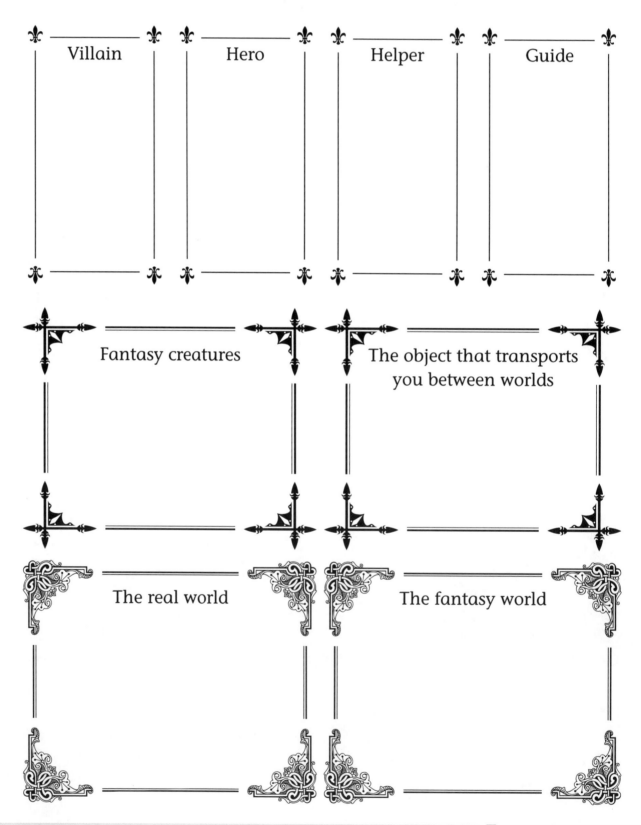

Villain

Hero

Helper

Guide

Fantasy creatures

The object that transports you between worlds

The real world

The fantasy world

The challenge or quest

The final showdown

Resolution and ending

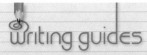

Review

These activities are designed to evaluate how effectively the children have incorporated the features of Sections 1 and 2 into their own writing. The children can use the self review and peer review sheets to assess their ongoing work during the drafting and editing process and/or to evaluate their completed stories. Teacher review should make an overall review of children's progress at the end of a unit of work on fantasy writing.

Self review

Photocopiable page 45 contains a checklist of typical structural, content and language features of the fantasy genre. The checklist is designed to be used by the children to review their own work. It is important to give each child a copy of the checklist to refer to when they are planning their fantasy story to ensure that they have a clear understanding of the success criteria that will be used to assess their work.

Ask the children to use the checklist to record how successfully they think they have incorporated the fantasy story features listed into their own writing (not at all, a little, quite well or very well).

Peer review

Peer review is an essential part of the review process. It develops the children's ability to work cooperatively and to give positive feedback.

The comment cards on photocopiable page 46 can be used by the children working in pairs (writing partners) or small groups (author circles) of similar ability. Ask the children to read and review each other's stories. Provide each child with a set of comment cards and ask them to note down what they think their partner has done well and how aspects of their writing could be developed/improved. Ensure that all feedback is constructive and supportive.

Teacher review

The teacher review table on photocopiable page 47 is modelled on the writing assessment guideline sheets produced by the DfES and can be used to assess the children's work against national standards for writing.

The table has been designed to enable you to assess pupils' progress and attainment at the end of a series of lessons on writing fantasy stories.

When reviewing children's ability in relation to each Assessment Focus, it is important to take into account a range of evidence collected, including observations (for example, of contributions made in discussion and drama), questioning and their extended stories.

The outcome of the teacher review should inform future planning, teaching and learning. The review may also highlight gaps in the children's experience and learning. If this is the case, revisit the relevant lesson/s in Section 2 of this *Writing Guide* to address these gaps.

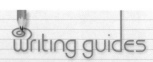

Self review

● Tick one of the boxes for each statement listed below.

		☹ Not at all	😐 A little	🙂 Quite well	😊 Very well
Characters	I introduce and develop typical fantasy characters in my story by describing what they do, how they feel and what they say.				
	I use dialogue at different points in my story.				
Setting	I give information about the time, place, climate and weather when describing the setting.				
	I describe how the setting makes the characters feel to create mood and atmosphere.				
Plot	The structure of my story includes: opening, build up, challenge, events, resolution and ending.				
	I have used paragraphs or chapters to organise my story into clear sections.				
Language	I use adjectives, adverbs, powerful verbs, similes and metaphors to describe people, places and events.				
	I use connecting words and phrases to join sentences and link paragraphs.				

I think I could improve my story by...

● _____

● _____

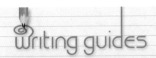

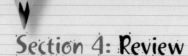

Peer review

● Use the comment cards below to review your partner's fantasy story.

My favourite *character* in your story is:

_____

_____

_____

You could develop this character even more by:

_____

_____

_____

Your *description* of _____

_____ is great.

You could make it even more interesting by:

_____

_____

_____

_____

My favourite *part* of your story is:

_____

_____

_____

You could make it even better by:

_____

_____

_____

I like the way you describe the *setting* by:

_____

_____

_____

You could make it even more effective by:

_____

_____

_____

Teacher review

	AF5 Vary sentences for clarity, purpose and effect.	AF6 Write with technical accuracy of syntax and punctuation in phrases, clauses and sentences.	AF3 Organise and present whole texts effectively, sequencing and structuring information, ideas and events.	AF4 Construct paragraphs and use cohesion within and between paragraphs.	AF1 Write imaginative, interesting and thoughtful texts.	AF2 Produce texts which are appropriate to the task, reader and purpose.	AF7 Select appropriate and effective vocabulary.
LEVEL 4	Some variation in sentence structure. *Use of some subordinating connectives throughout the text (QCA Assessment guidelines).*	Uses full stops, capital letters, exclamation marks and question marks accurately to punctuate sentences. Direct speech mostly correctly punctuated with speech marks.	The narrative is organised using a simple chronological structure.	Uses paragraph breaks to organise story content. *Use connecting words and phrases to give order and structure to writing (Year 5 Writing target).*	Content and ideas relevant to task. *Some ideas and material developed in detail, eg descriptions elaborated by adverbial and expanded noun phrases (QCA Assessment guidelines).*	Attempts to use appropriate narrative structure and style. Uses and adapts features of fantasy stories in own writing.	Uses vocabulary appropriate to task and audience. Some imaginative vocabulary choices used for effect.
LEVEL 5	Uses a range of simple, complex and compound sentence structures. *Wider range of connectives used to clarify relationship between ideas (QCA Assessment guidelines).*	*A full range of punctuation used accurately to demarcate sentences, including speech punctuation. (QCA Assessment guidelines).*	Some attempt to use more complex narrative structures and techniques. The story has a clear ending that refers back to the opening.	Story structured clearly with ideas organised into appropriate paragraphs or chapters. Uses a range of connectives within and between paragraphs to organise writing.	*Relevant ideas and material developed with some imaginative detail (QCA Assessment guidelines).* Engages the reader's interest through use of different narrative techniques.	Writing shows clear awareness of purpose and audience. Maintains narrative structure throughout.	Uses carefully selected vocabulary to create vivid descriptions of setting, characters and events. Some use of figurative language.

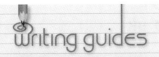

SCHOLASTIC

Also available in this series:

ISBN 978-1407-11253-4

ISBN 978-1407-11265-7

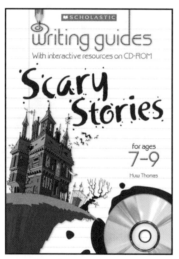

ISBN 978-1407-11267-1

ISBN 978-1407-11256-5

ISBN 978-1407-11270-1

ISBN 978-1407-11248-0

To find out more, call: **0845 603 9091**
or visit our website: **www.scholastic.co.uk**